Mix & Match MAMA
Simmers

SHAY SHULL

HARVEST HOUSE PUBLISHERS
EUGENE, OREGON

Cover by Kyler Dougherty
Interior design by Faceout Studio
Food photography by Shay Shull
Dedication photo © Shutterstock
All other photos by Jay Eads

Published in association with William K. Jensen Literary Agency,
119 Bampton Court, Eugene, Oregon 97404.

Mix and Match Mama® is a registered trademark of Mix and Match Mama, LLC

Mix-and-Match Simmers

Copyright © 2017 Mix and Match Mama
Published by Harvest House Publishers
Eugene, Oregon 97408
www.harvesthousepublishers.com

Library of Congress Cataloging-in-Publication Data

Names: Shull, Shay, 1981- author.
Title: Mix-and-Match Mama simmers / Shay Shull.
Description: Eugene, Oregon : Harvest House Publishers, [2017]
Identifiers: LCCN 2016053089 (print) | LCCN 2017000210 (ebook) | ISBN
    9780736968980 (pbk.) | ISBN 9780736968997 (e-book)
Subjects: LCSH: Quick and easy cooking. | LCGFT: Cookbooks.
Classification: LCC TX833.5 .S5344 2017 (print) | LCC TX833.5 (ebook) | DDC
    641.5/12--dc23
LC record available at https://lccn.loc.gov/2016053089

ISBN 978-0-7369-6898-0 (softcover)
ISBN 978-0-7369-6899-7 (ebook)

Printed in China

17 18 19 20 21 22 23 24 25 / RDS - FO / 10 9 8 7 6 5 4 3

To all of the Super Moms out there...

trying to get dinner on the table

every night for the ones you love.

Thank you for allowing me to

share my recipes with you.

xo

Contents

Introduction

I call it the Super Mom effect.

You know that moment when you come home tired after a long day and *bam!* There it is. Dinner. Cooked and simmering away on your counter because you had the foresight to throw a few ingredients in the slow cooker on your way out the door that morning. You are a superhero...you can get dinner done while you've been gone all day. The Super Mom effect. It's real, and it makes you feel good inside.

Other than my coffeepot, there is no kitchen appliance I use, love, and enjoy more than my slow cooker. It keeps my sanity on busy days, keeps my family's tummies fed when I'm just too tired and/or busy to cook, and it's my sidekick when I want to slow roast my favorite recipes.

I used to not like slow-cooked food because every recipe I tried was all brown and mushy looking and everything tasted about the same. But then I realized that if I just tweaked some of my favorite recipes, I could use my slow cooker to assist me in the kitchen. Sometimes the slow cooker does all the work, and I just remove the lid and enjoy. But other times it helps by doing most of the work for me, and then I just come in at the end of the day and add a few fresh ingredients before serving.

This book is filled with simple and unique ways to use your slow cooker to make your life easier. Let's all be Super Moms together.

Toppings, Tips, and Tricks

1. Buy a slow cooker that is oval and not round. You need one that will fit longer cuts of meats (such as roasts and briskets) and long spaghetti noodles. Round slow cookers just aren't as functional.

2. Buy a slow cooker with "high," "low," and "keep warm" settings. You'll be amazed at how much use you can get out of a slow cooker with all three settings (sometimes you have all day to cook, sometimes just a few hours, and sometimes you just need to keep your food warm until serving).

3. For dips and small appetizers, use a small slow cooker. Don't try to make a dip in a large slow cooker. Your slow cooker needs to be at least half full before using it...and a dip won't do that in a large slow cooker.

4. To me, a 6- to 7-quart slow cooker is ideal for dinners.

5. Always use a slow-cooker liner. Always. Every time. Never forget. They're sold next to the foil and Ziploc bags in the grocery store. They usually come five to a box. These babies will save you so much time and effort! Cleanup is a breeze if you use a liner. Always, always, always use one!

6. Always brown your beef before placing it in the slow cooker (yes, Mom, I'm talking to you!). Browning your meat beforehand adds so much more flavor and depth to the entire dish. It just takes a few minutes because you're not cooking it all the way through, you're just browning it—so do it! Chicken breasts do not require cooking beforehand, but ground meat (beef, chicken, or turkey), large roasts, or briskets do.

7. Add something fresh to your slow-cooker meal when you're done. I always add some fresh herbs, chopped green onions, cheese, or sour cream. Just a little something fresh on top wakens up the dish and gives the whole slow-cooker meal an extra *oomph*!

Perfect Chicken

I call it my "Perfect Chicken." This is my biggest slow-cooker tip...poach your chicken in advance for a variety of meals. Simply place boneless, skinless chicken breasts in your slow cooker with enough water to cover them (about 6 cups or so). Put on the lid and cook on low for 6 to 8 hours or on high for 3 to 4 hours. That's it! When you're ready to start cooking, simply remove the lid of your slow cooker, and the chicken will shred right up with just two forks. Discard the liquid and begin the recipe.

. . . .

Shay's Favorite Brisket

My favorite way to cook brisket is to brown both sides on the stove with a little olive oil and a bunch of sea salt and black pepper. After both sides are browned (only 3 or 4 minutes per side), I add the brisket to my slow cooker along with a 4-ounce bottle of liquid smoke and enough beef stock to cover the meat. I set my slow cooker to low and cook 6 to 10 hours. After that, I discard the liquid and the brisket is ready to eat!

. . . .

Tab's Guacamole

Many of the recipes in this book use Tab's Guacamole as a garnish. Tab is my bestie's husband, and he makes the world's best guacamole. Years ago, he was kind enough to share his recipe with me, and now we eat it almost every single night. Whenever you see Tab's Guacamole as a garnish in the book, refer to this recipe. Thank you, Tab!

INGREDIENTS

2 avocados, pits removed
½ red onion, chopped
1 clove garlic, chopped
1 jalapeño, chopped
1 tomato, chopped
Lots of salt (I love kosher or sea salt the best!)

In a medium-sized mixing bowl, combine all the ingredients, adding the salt to taste. Using a fork or potato masher, mash the mixture to desired consistency. (I prefer a chunky mixture, but you can mash this smooth if you like that best.)

Dips for Chips!

A slow-cooker staple is, of course, dips. You simply cannot have a slow-cooker book without adding in your favorite dip recipes.

Classic Queso

Cheesy Spinach Dip

Crab and Artichoke Dip

Spicy Corn Dip

Classic Queso

Everyone needs a basic queso recipe. This one right here will be in your slow cooker a lot. It's a classic worth repeating every single time.

This recipe serves six to eight.

INGREDIENTS

1 pound breakfast sausage (I use Owen's regular pork sausage. You can omit this step and make your dip vegetarian.)
1 (16 ounce) package Velveeta cheese
1 (10 ounce) can Ro-Tel tomatoes

In a large skillet over medium-high heat, brown the sausage until it's crumbly and cooked through. Place the sausage in your slow cooker. Add the Velveeta cheese (I cut mine into chunks to help it melt faster) and pour the tomatoes over the top. Cover and cook on high at least an hour before you remove the lid and stir. Once the dip is nice and melted, turn heat to low or "keep warm," and keep the device turned on as you enjoy your dip straight out of the slow cooker.

Cheesy Spinach Dip

All I did here was take the Classic Queso recipe and tweak it a little with spinach and extra green chilies. Now two favorite dips (spinach dip and queso) come together in one creamy slow-cooker recipe!

This recipe serves six to eight.

INGREDIENTS

1 (16 ounce) package Velveeta cheese
1 (10 ounce) can Ro-Tel tomatoes
2 (4 ounce) cans chopped green chilies
1 (10 ounce) package frozen spinach, thawed and drained of excess water

Place the Velveeta cheese (I cut mine into chunks to help it melt faster), tomatoes, and green chilies into your slow cooker. Cover and cook on high at least an hour before you remove the lid and stir. Once the dip is nice and melted, stir in the spinach. Continue cooking for another 15 to 20 minutes before turning heat to low or "keep warm" and continue to keep the device turned on as you enjoy your dip straight out of the slow cooker.

Crab and Artichoke Dip

A hot crab and artichoke dip is just a few steps away! For your next party, plug in your slow cooker and let it do all the work while you enjoy your guests.

This recipe serves six to eight.

INGREDIENTS

1 (12 ounce) can lump crab meat
1 (14 ounce) can quartered artichoke hearts, drained
2 tablespoons chili powder
2 (8 ounce) packages cream cheese, softened
½ cup milk
Good pinch of salt and pepper
Green onions for garnish, chopped

Place all the ingredients into the slow cooker except for the green onions. Allow the dip to cook on high for about an hour, or on low for about 3 hours. Stir to incorporate when ready to enjoy. When serving, garnish with the green onions.

Spicy Corn Dip

I can make a meal out of dip. Give me a yummy dip and some tortilla chips, and I am one happy camper. A dip with corn and bacon? Now, that's a really good meal!

This recipe serves six to eight.

INGREDIENTS

1 (8 ounce) package cream cheese, softened
2 (14 ounce) cans cream corn
2 (4 ounce) cans chopped green chilies
2 cups Pepper Jack cheese, shredded
2 cups frozen corn
Bacon for garnish, crumbled

Place the cream cheese, cream corn, green chilies, and Pepper Jack cheese into the slow cooker. Cover and cook on low for 2 to 3 hours. Remove the lid and stir until everything is nice and creamy.

Next, stir in the frozen corn and cook another 15 minutes or until the corn is heated through. Pour the dip into a bowl and garnish with bacon bits.

Perfect Chicken Recipes

Do you know how many recipes call for a pound of cooked and shredded chicken? A lot! When you get out your recipe for dinner and begin, the first step is to poach the chicken, allow it to cook, and then shred it. That takes so long! That step right there will delay your dinner by at least 30 minutes. My solution? Poach the chicken all day long while you're away, and then when you're ready to start supper, your chicken is ready and waiting on you. I call it my "Perfect Chicken." This chapter is dedicated to the many recipes that use my Perfect Chicken method (see page 9).

King Ranch Joes

Pineapple Lime
Chicken Tostadas

BBQ Chicken Taquitos

Spinach and Chicken
Enchiladas

Baked Chicken
and Spinach Tacos

Teriyaki Chicken Wraps

Honey Mustard Chicken
and Corn Wraps

Chicken Spaghetti

Tex-Mex Chicken Pot Pie

Ritzy Chicken Casserole

Sweet Corn and Chicken
over Wild Rice

Grape and Pecan
Chicken Salad

King Ranch Joes

The King Ranch Casserole reigns supreme in the South where I live...so I married it with another supper royalty—the sloppy joe—and created this masterpiece. Perfect Chicken from your slow cooker gets this meal on the table in no time.

This recipe serves four adults.

INGREDIENTS

1 pound Perfect Chicken, shredded (see page 9)
1 (10 ounce) can cream of mushroom soup
1 (10 ounce) can cream of chicken soup
1 (10 ounce) can Ro-Tel tomatoes
2 tablespoons chili powder
4 thick slices of corn bread for serving
Cheddar cheese for garnish, shredded
Green onions for garnish, chopped

Prepare a batch of Perfect Chicken. About an hour before you're ready to eat, discard the liquid and place the shredded chicken back into your slow cooker and turn it on to high. Stir in the cream soups, tomatoes, and chili powder. Cover and cook on high for 30 minutes to an hour.

When you're ready to serve, place a nice, thick piece of corn bread on each plate. Next, add a big dollop of the chicken mixture on top. Garnish with a little cheese and some green onions.

Pineapple Lime Chicken Tostadas

Pineapple and lime are a match made in heaven! Add them to Perfect Chicken with some guacamole, chopped jalapeño, and cilantro, and you have a restaurant-style dinner on the table in minutes. Your family will never believe this all started in the slow cooker.

This recipe serves four.

INGREDIENTS

1 pound Perfect Chicken, shredded (see page 9)
1 (20 ounce) can crushed pineapple
Zest and juice of one lime (about 2 tablespoons of each), reserving a little zest for serving
1 jalapeño, chopped (seed it if you would like less heat)
1 (10 ounce) can Ro-Tel tomatoes, drained
Tostada shells
Tab's Guacamole (see page 9)
Cilantro for garnish, chopped

In a mixing bowl, stir together the chicken, crushed pineapple, lime zest (remember to save a bit for later!), lime juice, jalapeño, and tomatoes.

Assemble your tostadas in this order: start with the shell and then add a generous portion of guacamole, some of the pineapple chicken mixture, and top with cilantro. Add just a touch of lime zest to the top to finish things off.

BBQ Chicken Taquitos

These little baked taquitos come together with your premade Perfect Chicken from the slow cooker. Everyone loves a taquito. All you do is assemble, bake, and enjoy!

This recipe makes six baked taquitos.

INGREDIENTS

6 flour tortillas
1 pound Perfect Chicken, shredded
(see page 9)
1 cup BBQ sauce
1 (15 ounce) can black beans,
drained and rinsed

1 cup corn kernels
About 8 green onions, chopped
1½ cups cooked rice (I use brown)
1 cup cheese, more or less (we use Queso
Fresco, but you could use Monterey Jack too)

Preheat oven to 400 degrees.

Line a baking sheet with foil and lightly spray with cooking spray for easy clean up. Lay all six tortillas flat on the baking sheet. Set aside.

In a mixing bowl, add the chicken and BBQ sauce. Stir to combine. Next, stir in the black beans, corn kernels, and green onions. Divide the rice evenly among the tortillas, spooning it down the middle of each one. Next, spoon the chicken and bean mixture down the middle of each tortilla. Finally, sprinkle on the cheese. Roll up each tortilla and place seam side down on the baking sheet.

Bake for about 20 minutes. When they start to brown and crisp just a little, remove from the oven and serve immediately.

Spinach and Chicken Enchiladas

I used to think enchiladas were too tricky for a weeknight supper...but I was wrong. When you let your chicken cook all day in the slow cooker, they're a cinch! Just come home, assemble, bake, and eat.

This recipe serves four.

INGREDIENTS

1 pound Perfect Chicken, shredded
(see page 9)
1 box frozen spinach, thawed and
drained of excess water
1 can cream of chicken soup

8 to 10 green onions, chopped
1 cup tomatillo or green chili salsa
6 flour tortillas (we use whole wheat)
1 cup Monterey Jack cheese, shredded

Preheat oven to 350 degrees.

Lightly spray an 8 x 8 baking dish with cooking spray. Set aside.

In a mixing bowl, combine the chicken, spinach, soup, most of the onions (save a few for garnish at the end), and a half cup of salsa.

Spoon the chicken mixture down the center of each tortilla. Roll the tortilla up and place seam side down in your baking dish. Repeat until all of the enchiladas are filled. Pour the remaining half cup of salsa over the tops of the enchiladas in the baking dish and sprinkle the cheese on top.

Bake for 30 minutes or until lightly brown and bubbly. Remove and garnish with a few extra pieces of green onion.

Baked Chicken and Spinach Tacos

Here's what I've learned in life...once you bake a taco, you can never go back. Tonight, use your Perfect Chicken and pull together these Baked Chicken and Spinach Tacos in no time flat.

This recipe serves four adults.

INGREDIENTS

1 pound Perfect Chicken, shredded (see page 9)
1 (10 ounce) package frozen spinach, thawed and drained of excess water
3 tablespoons chili powder
2 cups taco sauce or salsa
A handful of chopped cilantro
8 taco shells (I love the stand-and-stuff variety)
2 cups Monterey Jack cheese, shredded
Green onions for garnish, chopped
Tab's Guacamole for garnish (see page 9)

Preheat oven to 400 degrees.

Lightly spray an 8 x 8 baking dish with cooking spray. Set aside.

In a mixing bowl, combine the chicken, spinach, chili powder, taco sauce or salsa, and cilantro. Stuff each of the taco shells with the taco mixture. Place them in the prepared baking dish and sprinkle the cheese on top.

Bake about 16 to 18 minutes or until the cheese is bubbly and golden. Remove from oven, garnish with green onions and guacamole, and serve immediately.

Teriyaki Chicken Wraps

These Teriyaki Chicken Wraps make the perfect quick lunch or light supper. Toss everything together, add to a warmed tortilla, roll, and enjoy!

This recipe serves four.

INGREDIENTS

4 flour tortillas
1 pound Perfect Chicken, shredded (see page 9)
½ red bell pepper, chopped
1 red onion, chopped
1 (8 ounce) can pineapple pieces, drained
½ cup teriyaki sauce
Cilantro for garnish, chopped

Warm the tortillas in a clean, dry skillet for a few minutes per side or in the microwave.

In a mixing bowl, toss together the chicken, bell pepper, red onion, pineapple pieces, and teriyaki sauce. Divide the mixture evenly among the tortillas, spooning it down the middle of each one, and garnish with a bit of chopped cilantro. Roll them tightly and serve immediately.

Honey Mustard Chicken and Corn Wraps

I made these little wraps one day for lunch and then thought, *These would make a great dinner too!* Simple enough for lunch but hearty and yummy enough to serve for dinner.

This recipe makes 4 wraps. (Of course, you could make less if you're just serving yourself for lunch.)

INGREDIENTS

1 pound Perfect Chicken, shredded (see page 9)
1 cup or so of your favorite honey mustard salad dressing
1 cup corn kernels, frozen or fresh, at room temperature
6 to 8 green onions, chopped
About 2 cups of fresh spinach leaves
Pinch of salt and pepper
4 large tortillas (flour, corn, or whole wheat)

In a mixing bowl, combine the chicken with the honey mustard dressing, corn, and green onions. Add salt and pepper to taste.

Lay out the four tortillas and place a few spinach leaves down the center of each one. Spoon the chicken mixture over the spinach. Wrap up the tortillas, and you're ready for lunch.

So simple! I wrapped up my tortilla in a paper towel and then placed it in a baggie and headed off to the pool. The perfect little lunch and a great way to use up leftover chicken

Chicken Spaghetti

Every Texas girl has a chicken spaghetti recipe in her repertoire. This one uses a pound of Perfect Chicken, so that at the end of the day all you need to do is assemble and bake.

This recipe serves four to six.

INGREDIENTS

1 pound Perfect Chicken, shredded (see page 9)
1 (10 ounce) can Ro-Tel tomatoes
1 (4 ounce) can chopped green chilies
1 (16 ounce) package Velveeta cheese, cut into cubes
2 tablespoons chili powder
1 pound spaghetti noodles, cooked and drained
Cilantro for garnish, chopped

Preheat the oven to 350 degrees.

Grease a 9 x 13 baking dish with cooking spray. Set aside.

In a large pot over medium-high heat, mix together the chicken, tomatoes, green chilies, Velveeta, and chili powder. Stir the mixture until the Velveeta melts, and then add the cooked pasta and toss everything together. Pour this mixture into your prepared baking dish and bake for 20 to 25 minutes or until the edges are lightly browned and cheese is bubbling. Remove from the oven and serve with a sprinkle of cilantro.

Tex-Mex Chicken Pot Pie

We just love, love, love my chicken potpie. (Really, is there anything more comforting than chicken potpie? I think not.) So I decided to *mix and match* for a Tex-Mex version.

This recipe serves four adults.

INGREDIENTS

1 pound Perfect Chicken, shredded (see page 9)
1 small onion, chopped
1 green bell pepper, chopped
1 jalapeño, seeded and chopped (optional)
1 (10 ounce) can Ro-Tel tomatoes (do not drain)
1 (6 ounce) can tomato paste

1 tablespoon chili powder
1 cup chicken stock
1 cup frozen corn
Salt and pepper
1 can biscuits (I use Grands)
1 cup Cheddar cheese, shredded

Preheat the oven to 425 degrees.

Lightly spray an 8 x 8 baking dish with cooking spray. Set aside.

In a large skillet, combine the chicken, onion, bell pepper, jalapeño, tomatoes, tomato paste, chili powder, stock, and corn over medium-high heat. Add a pinch of salt and pepper and simmer for about five minutes.

Pour the chicken mixture into the prepared baking dish. Remove the biscuits from the can and lay them across the top of the chicken mixture. Sprinkle a little cheese on top.

Bake 8 to 10 minutes or until biscuits are brown and chicken mixture is bubbly. Remove from oven and serve.

Ritzy Chicken Casserole

Ritzy Chicken Casserole. A box of buttery crackers, some of our Perfect Chicken, and a supper dish your whole family will love!

This recipe serves four.

INGREDIENTS

1 pound Perfect Chicken, shredded (see page 9)
1 (10 ounce) can cream of mushroom soup
1 cup Parmesan cheese, grated
About 1 cup mushrooms, chopped (I like to use Portobello)
1 (10 ounce) box frozen spinach, thawed and drained of excess water

½ cup chicken stock (or water)
1½ tablespoons Italian seasoning blend
Salt and pepper
1 cup mozzarella cheese, grated
1 sleeve (about 35 crackers) Ritz crackers, lightly crushed
4 tablespoons butter, melted

Preheat oven to 400 degrees.

Lightly spray an 8 x 8 baking dish with cooking spray. Set aside.

In a large mixing bowl, combine the chicken, soup, Parmesan cheese, mushrooms, spinach, stock or water, Italian seasoning, and a generous pinch of both salt and pepper. Spread this mixture in the prepared baking dish. Sprinkle mozzarella cheese on top, and then sprinkle on the Ritz crackers. Drizzle melted butter over everything.

Bake for about 18 to 20 minutes, or until the sides are bubbly and the crackers lightly browned. Remove from oven and serve immediately.

Sweet Corn and Chicken over Wild Rice

I'm pretty much obsessed with any recipe that has corn in it. Corn, crispy bacon, chicken, and Parmesan cheese over wild rice? That's a meal worth coming home to!

This recipe serves four.

INGREDIENTS

1 shallot, chopped
Extra virgin olive oil
Salt and pepper
6 pieces bacon, chopped
1 (14 ounce) can cream corn
1 pound Perfect Chicken, shredded (see page 9)
1 cup Parmesan cheese, grated and divided
2 cups cooked wild rice

In a large skillet over medium-high heat, brown the shallot in a drizzle of extra virgin olive oil with a sprinkle of salt and pepper. Stir in the bacon and cook until crisp. Remove a few crispy bacon pieces to use for a garnish later. Next, stir in the cream corn and chicken. Toss everything together. Sprinkle in half of the Parmesan cheese. Simmer over low heat about five minutes until everything is heated through.

Place half a cup of wild rice in each of four serving dishes. Ladle on a helping of the chicken and corn mixture. Garnish with the remaining bacon and Parmesan cheese.

Grape and Pecan Chicken Salad

Oh, how I love chicken salad! I love it by itself, I love it in a sandwich...and I especially love it during spring and summer for lunch or a light supper. Another bonus? You can make it in advance. On those warm nights when you don't want to cook, you can pull some of this from the fridge and serve it with a slice of bakery bread, green salad, and wedge of watermelon and call it good. There are approximately 5 billion ways to make chicken salad, and I love each and every one of them. My favorite, though? One that has toasted pecans and sliced grapes mixed in. Delish! Use my Perfect Chicken, and this dish will be assembled in no time flat.

This recipe serves four.

INGREDIENTS

1 pound Perfect Chicken, shredded (see page 9)
About 2 cups grapes, sliced
About 2 cups toasted pecan pieces
About 8 to 10 green onions, chopped
1½ cups mayonnaise
1½ tablespoons Dijon mustard
Liberal pinch of both salt and pepper

In a mixing bowl, combine all of the ingredients. Make sure everything is nice and coated. Cover and refrigerate at least one hour or up to 24 hours. Remove from fridge, serve, and enjoy.

Soup-er Slow-Cooker Meals

Soups are the quintessential slow-cooker meal. A hearty bowl on a cold night just works every single time. These are a few of my very favorite soup recipes that always warm us, heart and soul.

Chicken Enchilada Quinoa Soup

Santa Fe Soup

Taco Tortellini Soup

Chicken Tortilla Soup

Mama's Minestrone

Italian Wedding Soup

Potato Soup

Hash Brown Chicken Corn Chowder

Chicken Noodle Soup

White Bean, Kale, and Sausage Soup

Brunswick Stew

Chicken Enchilada Quinoa Soup

I wanted to make a soup that tasted like an enchilada, had quinoa in it, and was made in the slow cooker. Done, done, and done. You place everything in the slow cooker. Turn it on, walk away, and come back later to the most delicious dinner your family has had in ages. I'm telling you, make this tonight. You'll thank me! Make sure you run your quinoa under cold water to rinse it off before using. Rinse and then shake the excess water out before adding into soup.

This recipe serves four adults.

INGREDIENTS

1 pound boneless, skinless chicken breasts
1 (15 ounce) can ranch-style beans (do not drain)
1½ cups quinoa (rinsed and drained)
1 (14 ounce) can enchilada sauce (I use mild)
1 (10 ounce) can Ro-Tel tomatoes
1 (4 ounce) can chopped green chilies
2 cups chicken stock
Salt and pepper
Green onions for garnish, chopped
Cheddar cheese for garnish, shredded

Place the chicken breasts, beans, quinoa, enchilada sauce, tomatoes, chilies, stock, and a big pinch of salt and pepper in the bottom of the slow cooker. Cover and cook on low for 6 to 8 hours or on high for 3 to 4 hours.

When you're ready to eat, remove the lid and shred the chicken inside the slow cooker using two forks. Next, ladle the soup into bowls and garnish it with green onions and cheese.

Santa Fe Soup

Soups like these are my favorite. Everything goes into the slow cooker. And then at the end of the day, dinner is not only done...it's delicious! Happy soup night!

This recipe serves four.

INGREDIENTS

1 pound uncooked chicken breasts
1 (15 ounce) can black beans, rinsed and drained
1 (10 ounce) can Ro-Tel tomatoes
1 (14 ounce) can cream corn
1 (4 ounce) can chopped green chilies
2 cups chicken stock
2 tablespoons chili powder
Monterey Jack cheese for garnish, shredded
Green onions for garnish, chopped

Place the chicken breasts, beans, tomatoes, cream corn, chilies, stock, and chili powder in the bottom of the slow cooker. Cover and cook on low for 6 to 8 hours or on high for 3 to 4 hours. When you're ready to serve, remove the lid and shred chicken right inside your slow cooker using two forks. Ladle the soup into bowls and garnish with the cheese and green onions.

Taco Tortellini Soup

This soup is what I call a "one-pound meal." That means, even though I use a pound of ground beef, you can easily substitute ground chicken or ground turkey instead.

This recipe serves four.

INGREDIENTS

1 pound ground beef
Extra virgin olive oil
Salt and pepper
1 onion, chopped
1 (1 ounce) packet taco seasoning
1 (10 ounce) can Ro-Tel tomatoes
2 cups chicken stock

1 (15 ounce) can black beans, rinsed and drained
1 (8 ounce) can tomato sauce
2 (9 ounce) packages refrigerated cheese tortellini (I use Buitoni)
1½ cups frozen corn
Cheddar cheese for garnish, shredded

In a skillet over medium-high heat, brown the ground beef in a little drizzle of olive oil. Once it's brown and crumbly, add a pinch of salt and pepper and then transfer the ground beef to your slow cooker.

Next, add the onion, taco seasoning, tomatoes, stock, beans, and tomato sauce. Cover and cook on low for 6 to 8 hours or on high for 3 to 4 hours. About 30 minutes before you're ready to serve, remove the lid and add the tortellini and frozen corn. Cover and cook on high for 30 minutes. When ready to serve, ladle the soup into bowls, garnish with a little cheese, and serve.

Chicken Tortilla Soup

This recipe right here will probably be the one you refer to the most in this book. A classic chicken tortilla soup recipe that just cannot be beaten. It's always on point.

This recipe serves four.

INGREDIENTS

1 pound boneless, skinless chicken breasts
1 (10 ounce) can Ro-Tel tomatoes
1 (14 ounce) can diced tomatoes
1 (14 ounce) can ranch-style beans
1 (1 ounce) packet taco seasoning
1 (10 ounce) can cream of chicken soup
2 cups corn kernels, fresh or frozen
Monterey Jack cheese for garnish, shredded
Green onions for garnish, chopped

In the slow cooker, layer the chicken, tomatoes, beans, taco seasoning, and cream of chicken soup. Cover and cook on low for 6 to 8 hours or on high for 3 to 4 hours. About 20 minutes before you're ready to serve, remove the lid and stir in the corn. Replace the lid and heat until the corn is hot. Ladle the soup into bowls and garnish with cheese and green onions.

Mama's Minestrone

This soup is so hearty and filling that the carnivores in your family will never even miss the meat!

This recipe serves four.

INGREDIENTS

1 (15 ounce) can kidney beans, rinsed and drained
1 (15 ounce) can Great Northern beans, rinsed and drained
1 (14 ounce) can diced tomatoes
1 (6 ounce) can tomato paste
1 onion, chopped
1 (1 ounce) packet dry ranch seasoning mix
2 cups chicken stock
Salt and pepper
1 (10 ounce) package frozen vegetable medley (I use carrots and squash)
1 pound short cut pasta (I use elbow noodles)
Parsley for garnish, chopped
Parmesan cheese for garnish, grated

Add the beans, tomatoes, tomato paste, onion, ranch seasoning mix, and stock along with a hearty pinch of salt and pepper to your slow cooker. Cover and cook on low 6 to 8 hours or on high 3 to 4 hours. About 30 minutes before you're ready to eat, remove the lid and stir in the frozen vegetables and pasta. Cover and cook on high for another 20 to 30 minutes. Remove the lid and ladle into bowls. Serve with a garnish of parsley and a little Parmesan.

Italian Wedding Soup

This is my easy weeknight spin on a classic. So much goodness in every bowl.

This recipe serves four.

INGREDIENTS

1 (1 pound) bag frozen meatballs
1 onion, chopped
4 cups beef stock
2 teaspoons garlic powder
1 (15 ounce) can tomato sauce
1 (14 ounce) can diced tomatoes
1 (10 ounce) box frozen spinach, thawed
and drained of excess water
1 (10 ounce) package frozen carrots
1 box (about 4 cups or so) small pasta
Parmesan cheese for garnish, grated
Cilantro or parsley for garnish, chopped

In the slow cooker, mix together the meatballs, onion, beef stock, garlic powder, tomato sauce, and diced tomatoes. Cover and cook on low for 6 to 7 hours or on high for 3 to 4 hours. About 20 minutes before you're ready to eat, stir in the spinach, carrots, and pasta. Cover and turn the slow cooker to high for the last 20 minutes. When you're ready to serve, ladle the soup into bowls and garnish with Parmesan cheese and either a little cilantro or parsley.

Potato Soup

On a chilly night, the most comforting thing is, of course, potato soup. I use frozen hash browns in my recipe for a quick-cooking, easy-to-prepare, creamy, yummy bowl of goodness.

This recipe serves four.

INGREDIENTS

1 (32 ounce) bag frozen cubed hash brown potatoes
1 onion, chopped
8 slices raw bacon, chopped, and divided
2 cups milk
2 cups chicken stock
Salt and pepper
Green onions for garnish, chopped
Cheddar cheese for garnish, shredded

In the slow cooker, place the frozen hash browns, onion, 4 slices of bacon pieces (reserve the other pieces for later), milk, stock, and a big pinch of both salt and pepper. Cover and cook on low for 6 to 8 hours or on high for 3 to 4 hours. Right before serving, cook the remaining pieces of bacon in a skillet until crisp. Pat them dry with a paper towel and then crumble them. Ladle soup into bowls and garnish with the bacon crumbles, green onions, and cheese.

Hash Brown Chicken Corn Chowder

This chicken soup is prepared in the slow cooker all day so that when dinnertime comes, your meal is ready and waiting on you. And, bonus, frozen hash browns make this even more filling and quick to pull together!

This recipe serves four.

INGREDIENTS

1 pound boneless, skinless chicken breasts
1 onion, chopped
2 (14 ounce) cans cream corn
1 (4 ounce) can chopped green chilies
2 cups chicken stock
2 tablespoons chili powder
4 cups frozen diced hash browns
Cheddar cheese for garnish, shredded

In your slow cooker, place chicken, onion, cream corn, chilies, stock, and chili powder. Stir in hash browns. Cover and cook on low for 6 to 8 hours or on high for 3 to 4 hours. When you're ready to serve, remove the lid and shred the chicken right inside your slow cooker using two forks. Ladle the soup into bowls and garnish with cheese.

Chicken Noodle Soup

A hearty bowl of chicken and noodles is like medicine for your soul.

This recipe serves four.

INGREDIENTS

1 pound boneless, skinless chicken breasts
1 onion, chopped
1 (10 ounce) can cream of chicken soup
1 (14 ounce) can cream corn
2 cups chicken stock
Salt and pepper
1 (10 ounce) package frozen vegetable medley (carrots and peas work great)
1 pound small pasta (I use elbow noodles)
Parsley for garnish, chopped

In the slow cooker, place the chicken, onion, soup, cream corn, stock, and a hearty pinch of salt and pepper. Cover and cook on low for 6 to 8 hours or on high for 3 to 4 hours. About 30 minutes before you're ready to eat, remove the lid and shred the chicken right inside the slow cooker using two forks. Next, stir in the vegetables and pasta. Cover and cook on high for another 20 to 30 minutes. Remove the lid and ladle the soup into bowls with a garnish of parsley.

White Bean, Kale, and Sausage Soup

Thanks to the potatoes, this soup is extra thick and hearty. So much flavor, one little bowl.

This recipe serves four.

INGREDIENTS

1 pound sausage, browned and crumbly (I use Italian-style sausage)
1 (15 ounce) can Great Northern beans, rinsed and drained
4 cups kale, torn into pieces
2 russet potatoes, peeled and chopped into bite-sized pieces
1 onion, chopped
2 cloves garlic, minced
1 tablespoon Dijon mustard
About 2 cups of chicken stock
Splash of heavy cream or half-and-half
Cheddar cheese for garnish, shredded

Layer the sausage in the bottom of the slow cooker, and then add the beans, kale, potatoes, onion, garlic, and mustard. Pour chicken stock over everything. Cover and cook for 6 to 8 hours on low or for 3 to 4 hours on high. When you're ready to serve, remove the lid and stir in a splash of cream. Ladle the soup into bowls and garnish with cheese.

Brunswick Stew

This slow cooker fave uses pork tenderloin as the protein. A hearty bowl on a cold day alongside some crusty bread and salad, dinner is done.

This meals serves four to six.

INGREDIENTS

1 (2 pounds) pork tenderloin
1 onion, chopped
1 (8 ounce) can tomato sauce
1 (14 ounce) can diced tomatoes
1 cup BBQ sauce
1 cup chicken stock
1 (14 ounce) can cream corn
1 cup frozen lima beans
2 cups frozen peas and carrots mix
1 cup frozen corn

Add the first seven ingredients to the slow cooker. Cover and cook on low for 8 to 10 hours or on high for 4 to 5 hours.

About 30 minutes before you're ready to serve, remove the lid and shred the pork right inside the slow cooker using two forks. After the pork is shredded, stir in the beans and veggies. Cover again and cook on high for 30 minutes. Remove the lid and ladle the soup into bowls.

Brown and Go

First you brown, then you go! These recipes require just one step before putting everything in the slow cooker—browning. Browning some cuts of meat is an essential step when using the slow cooker. Beef in particular needs to be browned before added in. I brown mine while I sip my coffee and catch up on the morning news. After that, I just add it to my slow cooker plus the other ingredients, and I'm off and running.

Beef Enchilada Tacos

Brisket Nachos

Chipotle Turkey Chili

Mexican Lettuce Wraps

Brisket Ranch Sandwiches

Brisket and Bacon
Grilled Cheese

French Onion Joes

Old-Fashioned Sloppy Joes

Slow-Cooker Stroganoff

Beef Enchilada Tacos

Tacos are probably the number one thing we make in the slow cooker at my house. They're so simple, everyone can build their own, and they're always a hit. The next time you have Taco Tuesday, make it with these slow-cooker Beef Enchilada Tacos.

This recipe serves four.

INGREDIENTS

1½ pounds ground beef, browned and crumbly
1 (10 ounce) can enchilada sauce (we use mild)
1 (16 ounce) can chili beans
About 8 flour tortillas
Romaine lettuce
Tab's Guacamole (see page 9)
Pepper or Monterey Jack cheese, shredded
Green onions for garnish, chopped

Place the browned ground beef in the bottom of the slow cooker. Next, stir in the enchilada sauce and chili beans. Cover and cook on low for 6 to 8 hours or on high for 3 to 4 hours.

When you're ready to serve, take a tortilla (I like to warm mine in the microwave for about 20 seconds between two damp paper towels before filling) and top it with the lettuce, a little guacamole, the ground beef mixture, a sprinkle of cheese, and the green onions.

Brisket Nachos

Is there anything simpler or more fun to eat than nachos? A pile of chips topped with cheese and yummy brisket (plus some deli jalapeños for a little kick!). When my hubby was in college, my favorite place to eat when I would go visit him was a BBQ joint that served the most delicious Brisket Nachos. This is my version of that favorite supper.

This recipe serves four.

INGREDIENTS

1 bag of your favorite tortillas chips
1 pound beef brisket, shredded
About 2 cups Cheddar cheese, shredded (see page 9)
About 8 green onions, chopped
Deli jalapeños for garnish, sliced

Preheat the oven to 400 degrees.

Lightly spray a 9 x 13 baking dish or several individual baking dishes with cooking spray. Layer the chips across the bottom of the baking dish. Next, add the brisket on top of the chips, and then the Cheddar cheese and green onions.

Bake about 12 to 15 minutes or until the cheese is bubbly and melted and the chips are nicely browned. Remove from oven and garnish with the deli jalapeños.

Chipotle Turkey Chili

I simply cannot have enough chili recipes for my slow cooker. This particular recipe is made with ground turkey, but ground beef works too. Do not be afraid of the chipotle peppers...they'll give this recipe a lot of flavor with very little heat.

This recipe serves four.

INGREDIENTS

1 pound ground turkey
Extra virgin olive oil
Salt and pepper
1 onion, chopped
1 small can chipotle peppers in adobo sauce
(you'll only need 2 peppers and a little sauce!)
1 (14 ounce) can diced tomatoes
1 (6 ounce) can tomato paste

2 cups chicken stock
1 (15 ounce) can black beans, rinsed and drained
3 tablespoons chili powder
1½ cups frozen corn
Monterey Jack cheese for garnish, shredded
Sour cream for garnish (optional)
Cilantro for garnish, chopped (optional)

In a large skillet over medium-high heat, brown the ground turkey in a drizzle of olive oil. Once browned add a big pinch of salt and pepper and transfer to your slow cooker.

Next, layer the onion, two chipotle peppers (or a few more for extra heat) along with a little adobo sauce, tomatoes, tomato paste, stock, beans, and chili powder. Cover and cook on low for 6 to 8 hours or on high for 3 to 4 hours. About 20 minutes before you're ready to serve, remove the lid and stir in the corn. Continue on high and for 20 minutes. Garnish with cheese, sour cream, and cilantro.

Mexican Lettuce Wraps

I'm calling these Mexican Lettuce Wraps, but, really, they're like tacos without the tortilla shell. The filling simmers away all day in your slow cooker, and then you wrap, top, and roll come dinner time.

This recipe makes eight wraps to serve four people.

INGREDIENTS

1 pound ground beef
Extra virgin olive oil
Salt and pepper
2 tablespoons chili powder
1 (15 ounce) can chili beans
1 (10 ounce) can Ro-Tel tomatoes
About 8 large lettuce leaves
Tab's Guacamole for garnish (see page 9)
Pepper Jack cheese for garnish, shredded
Green onion for garnish, chopped

In a skillet over medium-high heat, brown ground beef in a drizzle of olive oil. Once browned and crumbly, stir in a big pinch of both salt and pepper and the chili powder. Pour this mixture into your slow cooker, and then add the chili beans and tomatoes. Cover and cook on low for 6 to 8 hours or on high for 3 to 4 hours. When you're ready to serve, take a lettuce leaf and add a big dollop of meat to each one followed by your favorite garnishes.

Brisket Ranch Sandwiches

Brisket browns all day and then a quick sandwich is assembled at dinner.

This recipe serves four to six.

INGREDIENTS

1 brisket (2 pounds), flat and trimmed
2 tablespoons extra virgin olive oil
Salt and pepper
1 (4 ounce) bottle of liquid smoke (use either hickory or mesquite flavored)
4 cups beef stock
4 to 6 hoagie rolls, split in half
Several handfuls of romaine lettuce
2 avocados, peeled and sliced
Your favorite ranch salad dressing
1 red onion, chopped

In a large pot over medium-high heat, brown both sides of the brisket in two table-spoons olive oil. Salt and pepper each side of the brisket quite liberally. After each side is browned (about 3 minutes per side), place the brisket in the slow cooker along with the entire bottle of liquid smoke and the beef stock. Cover and cook on low for 8 hours or on high for 4 hours.

When you're ready to assemble your sandwiches, remove the brisket from the slow cooker (discard all liquid) and slice the meat. For each dinner roll, add some romaine lettuce, sliced brisket, avocado, red onion, and a drizzle of ranch salad dressing.

Brisket and Bacon Grilled Cheese

Some nights you just need a big old bite of comfort food. I took my favorite brisket and turned it into this insanely delicious grilled cheese sandwich with bacon. *With bacon.* Brisket, bacon, cheese, and crusty bread...if that's not comfort food, I don't know what is.

This recipe serves four.

INGREDIENTS

1 pound beef brisket, cooked and shredded (see page 9)
About 2 cups BBQ sauce
8 slices bacon, cooked until crispy
2 cups Cheddar cheese, shredded
8 slices of good quality French bread (or whatever bread you love!)
About 2 tablespoons butter

Preheat a large skillet or griddle to medium-high heat.

In a mixing bowl, combine the shredded brisket and BBQ sauce. Set aside.

Lay out four slices of bread. Top each slice with two pieces of cooked and crispy bacon. Next, add a big scoop of the BBQ brisket and then top with shredded cheese. Place another slice of bread on top and get ready to grill.

Add the butter to the hot griddle or skillet and allow to melt. One at a time, add your sandwiches and slightly press down with a spatula. After a few minutes, flip them over and brown the other side. Remove from grill, slice in half, and serve immediately.

French Onion Joes

It's a sloppy joe that tastes like French Onion Soup. Basically, it's perfect.

This recipe serves four.

INGREDIENTS

1 pound ground beef
Extra virgin olive oil
Salt and pepper
2 onions, chopped
3 cups beef stock

1 tablespoon Dijon mustard
3 tablespoons Worcestershire sauce
Sourdough bread, sliced thick
2 cups Gruyere cheese, shredded
Parsley for garnish, chopped

In a large skillet over medium-high heat, brown the ground beef in a drizzle of olive oil. Once browned, add a big pinch of both salt and pepper before transferring the meat to your slow cooker. Next, add the onions, beef stock, Dijon, and Worcestershire sauce. Cover with a lid and cook on high for 3 to 4 hours or on low for 6 to 8 hours.

About 15 minutes before you're ready to eat, preheat your oven to 425 degrees. On a baking sheet, lay out four slices of sourdough bread. Remove the lid from your slow cooker and ladle a generous portion of the ground beef on top of each piece of bread. Sprinkle with cheese and bake for about 10 minutes or until the cheese is nice and melted. Remove from the oven and garnish with parsley before serving.

Old-Fashioned Sloppy Joes

You just can't beat an old-fashioned sloppy joe. My version simmers all day in the slow cooker and then is ready and waiting come suppertime.

This recipe serves four.

INGREDIENTS

1 pound ground beef
Extra virgin olive oil
Large pinch of both salt and pepper
1 (6 ounce) can tomato paste
1 (8 ounce) can tomato sauce
1 (14 ounce) can diced tomatoes
3 tablespoons Worcestershire sauce
1 tablespoon mustard
3 tablespoons brown sugar
4 burger buns
Green onions for garnish, chopped

In a large skillet over medium-high heat, brown the ground beef in a drizzle of olive oil. Once browned and crumbly, add in a liberal pinch of both salt and pepper before transferring the meat to your slow cooker. Next, add the tomato paste, tomato sauce, tomatoes, Worcestershire sauce, mustard, and brown sugar. Stir and then cover with the lid and cook on low for 6 to 8 hours or on high for 3 hours. When you're ready to serve, add a generous scoop of sloppy joe mixture to the burger buns and garnish with green onions.

Slow-Cooker Stroganoff

Cozy up with a big bowl of this yummy stroganoff and watch your favorite show on TV. Make sure you're wearing your fuzzy socks. Fuzzy socks just seem to go with a cozy dinner like this.

This recipe serves four.

INGREDIENTS

1½ to 2 pounds stew meat
1 tablespoon extra virgin olive oil
Salt and pepper
1 onion, chopped
1 can beef broth
1 can cream of mushroom soup
1 (8 ounce) package cream cheese, softened
2 tablespoons Worcestershire sauce
1 teaspoon garlic powder
1 pound egg noodles
Parsley for garnish, chopped

Over medium-high heat, brown the stew meat in a tablespoon of olive oil and some salt and pepper (about 5 minutes). Transfer meat to your slow cooker. Add the onion, broth, cream of mushroom soup, cream cheese, Worcestershire sauce, and garlic powder. Cover and cook on low for 6 hours or on high for 3 hours.

About 30 minutes before you're ready to eat, turn the heat to high and add the noodles. Continue cooking, uncovered, until noodles are tender (about 30 minutes). Sprinkle on chopped parsley for garnish.

Andrea's Pulled Pork and Other Great Pork Recipes

One of my very best friends, Andrea, gave me her amazing BBQ Pulled Pork recipe years ago, and it's a staple in our kitchen. This recipe is so simple, so versatile, and so delicious every single time. What I love the most about this pulled pork is that you can make a double batch and enjoy the leftovers the next night in a completely different recipe. There is no other recipe I make more in my slow cooker than this one. Thank you, sweet friend, for sharing your recipe with me...and for the many laughs we've had around your kitchen table.

Andrea's Pulled Pork
Sandwiches

Pulled Pork Enchiladas

BBQ Pork Rice Bowls

BBQ Goat Cheese Pizza

Pork and Beans over Rice

BBQ Quesadillas

Pulled Pork Tacos

Andrea's Pulled Pork Sandwiches

This recipe right here is one of my very favorites. It requires only four ingredients, you put them all in the slow cooker, and then you leave them alone until you're ready to eat. This is the *perfect* meal to make on busy school days (during the fall, we eat it almost weekly). And it makes up a huge batch, so you can even have it two nights in a row if you like. What I have learned over the years is that this recipe is excellent for another reason too—it lends itself to many more delicious suppers. Whether you make up a big batch of this and keep the leftovers for another recipe the next night, or you just make this pork and go straight into another recipe, either way, the pork shines bright.

If you use a 3- to 5-pound piece of pork, you could easily get 6 to 8 servings out of this one recipe.

INGREDIENTS

1 (3 to 5 pounds) pork shoulder, pork butt, or pork tenderloin
1 large onion, chopped into big chunks
2 cans soda (not diet—I have used both Coca-Cola and Dr Pepper)
1 (12 to 18 ounce) bottle of your favorite BBQ Sauce (Andrea and I use Sweet Baby Ray's)
Green onions for garnish (optional), chopped
Buns if you're making sandwiches

Place the pork and onion pieces in the bottom of the slow cooker. Pour the soda over the meat and onions, cover the slow cooker, and cook on high for at least 8 to 10 hours.

When you remove the lid after the cooking time, the meat should be falling apart at the touch of your fork. Remove all of the meat from the slow cooker into a bowl and then discard the onions and liquid. Add the meat back into the slow cooker and shred it with two forks. Stir in as much BBQ sauce as you like. At this point, you can serve immediately, or you can turn the slow cooker to the "keep warm" setting and let it stay warm for up to 4 or 5 hours until you're ready to eat.

BBQ Goat Cheese Pizza

Two of my very favorite things come together in one delicious pizza: BBQ pulled pork and goat cheese. I mean to tell you...this dish right here will not disappoint. This is the kind of recipe you could make for your family on a weeknight and then again for a crowd over the weekend. Sure to please and always impress!

This recipe serves four.

INGREDIENTS

1 red onion, chopped
Extra virgin olive oil
Salt and pepper
Either homemade pizza dough or one premade pizza crust

About 2 cups of your favorite BBQ sauce
About 1 pound Andrea's Pulled Pork (see page 73)
About 1 cup fresh basil, chopped
About 8 ounces fresh goat cheese

Preheat oven to 425 degrees.

In a large skillet over medium-high heat, sauté the onion in a drizzle of olive oil along with a big pinch of salt and pepper, about 7 to 8 minutes or until tender. While your onion is sautéing, spread the pizza crust with BBQ sauce. Next, spread the pulled pork over the sauce. Remove the onion from the skillet and spread it across the top of the pizza followed by the basil. Bake about 15 minutes or until the edge is nicely browned and the sauce is bubbly.

Remove from the oven and immediately sprinkle the goat cheese across the top. Slice into wedges, serve, and enjoy.

BBQ Quesadillas

The key to these quesadillas are the pickles. Trust me...the pickles are the key. Make up a batch of Andrea's Pulled Pork or use leftovers. Delish!

This recipe makes about 8 big quesadillas (and then you split each of them in half).

INGREDIENTS

1 batch of Andrea's Pulled Pork (see page 73)
½ red onion, chopped
About a cup of dill pickle slices, drained of juice and chopped
About a cup (depending on how many you're making) of Monterey Jack cheese, shredded
Extra BBQ sauce (I use Sweet Baby Ray's)
Big flour tortillas (the "burrito" sized ones work best)

Preheat an indoor griddle or a big skillet to medium-high heat. Spray lightly with cooking spray.

Lay out however many flour tortillas you're going to use. Spread the pulled pork evenly among the tortillas, spooning it across the bottom half of each one. Add the red onion, pickles, and cheese on top of the pork. Drizzle just a bit more BBQ sauce on each tortilla if desired. Fold the top part down to cover the bottom portion.

Place each quesadilla in the skillet one at a time. Brown on both sides, cooking about 4 minutes or so on each side. When done, remove and slice in half (to give you two quesadillas); keep warm while browning the rest of the quesadillas.

Pulled Pork Tacos

Oh, mercy. I could probably eat these tacos every single night for dinner. You take some green onions and lay them across the bottom of a taco shell, add a generous scoop of Andrea's Pulled Pork and some cheese, and bake. Then, just when you think things can't get better...you add a dollop of guacamole on top. Perfection.

This recipe makes eight tacos to serve four people.

INGREDIENTS

8 taco shells (I like the stand-and-stuff shells for baking)
About 24 green onions
1 pound Andrea's Pulled Pork (see page 73)
2 cups Monterey Jack cheese, shredded
Tab's Guacamole for garnish (see page 9)

Lightly spray an 8x8 baking dish with cooking spray. Set a side. Preheat oven to 350 degrees.

Lightly grease a 9 x 13 baking dish with cooking spray. Stand the taco shells up inside of the baking dish. Next, place about 3 to 4 green onions on the bottom of each shell. After that, add some pulled pork (the pork can be right out of the slow cooker or out of the fridge if you're using leftovers). Finally, sprinkle cheese across the tops of each taco.

Bake the tacos for about 15 to 18 minutes or until the shells are nice and crispy, the pork is hot, and the cheese is melted and browned just a bit. Remove from oven and dollop each taco with guacamole. Serve immediately.

Pulled Pork Enchiladas

In this recipe, we'll take Andrea's Pulled Pork and turn it into yummy enchiladas. Taco sauce, corn, green onions, shredded Cheddar cheese...the makings of a delicious dinner!

This recipe serves four.

INGREDIENTS

About 1 pound Andrea's Pulled Pork (see page 73)
2 (10 ounce) cans enchilada sauce
8 flour tortillas
2 cups corn kernels, fresh or frozen
About 8 green onions, chopped (reserve some for garnish)
About 2 cups Cheddar cheese (reserve some for garnish), shredded

Preheat oven to 350 degrees.

Lighty grease an 8 x 8 baking dish. Set aside.

In a mixing bowl, toss together Andrea's Pulled Pork with one can of enchilada sauce. Now, take each tortilla and spoon some of this meat mixture across the center of each one. Next, add the corn, green onions, and cheese. Roll up each tortilla and place it seam side down in your baking dish. Once all of the enchiladas have been rolled up and placed in the dish, pour the second can of enchilada sauce over the tops of them.

Bake for about 20 minutes or until the edges of the enchiladas are nicely browned and the sauce is bubbly. Remove from oven and serve with a garnish of green onions and cheese.

BBQ Pork Rice Bowls

We love rice bowls around our house. Everyone fills their bowl with their favorite toppings, and then we sit down to a cozy dinner. Rice, pulled pork, some creamy avocado, and corn. Dinner is done!

This recipe serves four.

INGREDIENTS

1 pound Andrea's Pulled Pork (see page 73)
About 1 cup cooked corn kernels, warm or at room temperature (not frozen)
2 avocados, peeled and diced
About 8 green onions, chopped
About 4 cups rice, cooked and ready to eat (we use brown rice)

Place the pulled pork in a large mixing bowl and stir in the corn.

Take each serving bowl and add about a cup of rice to each one. Top the rice with the BBQ pork and corn mixture. Then, top everything with avocado and green onions.

Pork and Beans over Rice

My little version of pork and beans...and when cooked in the slow cooker, it's extra simple!

This recipe serves four to six.

INGREDIENTS

1 batch of Andrea's Pulled Pork (see page 73)
2 cups ketchup
¼ cup brown sugar
1 tablespoon apple cider vinegar
2 teaspoons garlic powder
1 tablespoon mustard
1 (15 ounce) can black beans, drained and rinsed
1 (15 ounce) can kidney beans, drained and rinsed
Green onions for garnish, chopped
About 4 cups cooked rice (white, brown...any kind!)

Prepare Andrea's Perfect Pulled Pork.

About 30 minutes to an hour before you're ready to eat, remove the pork from the slow cooker. Drain the liquid and then add the pork back in. Take two forks and shred the pork right inside the slow cooker. Next, add the ketchup, brown sugar, apple cider vinegar, garlic powder, mustard, and both cans of beans. Stir well. Cover and cook on high for 30 minutes to an hour.

When you're ready to serve, add rice to each plate, and then top the rice with the shredded pork and garnish with the green onions.

Other Slow-Cooker Staples

This chapter is dedicated to those other slow-cooker recipes we just love to make. Assemble before your day begins, and enjoy the fruits of your labor that night.

BBQ Ranch Chicken Sandwiches

Apple Cider Pork Tenderloin

Chicken and Mushrooms over Rice

Cheesy Chicken Pasta

Slow-Cooker Spaghetti and Meatballs

Sweet and Tangy Meatballs over Rice

BBQ Ranch Chicken Sandwiches

I'm always thinking of ways to create hearty suppers in the slow cooker that don't taste like "slow cooker meals." My BBQ Ranch Chicken Sandwiches are just that! You pile the ingredients in the slow cooker first thing in the morning, let them cook all day, come home, crisp up some bacon bits for garnish, assemble, and enjoy. That's it! This is a family meal you can eat year around.

This recipe serves four.

INGREDIENTS

1 pound boneless, skinless chicken breasts
1 bottle of your favorite BBQ sauce (enough sauce to completely cover the chicken in the slow cooker, about 3 cups or so)
1 (1 ounce) packet ranch dressing mix
4 burger buns
Ranch salad dressing for garnish
Green onions for garnish, chopped
Bacon for garnish (I use four slices), chopped and cooked crisp

Place the chicken, BBQ sauce, and packet of dry ranch dressing mix in the slow cooker. Cover and cook on low for 6 to 8 hours or on high for 3 to 4 hours.

When you're ready to serve, remove the lid and shred the chicken right inside of the slow cooker using two forks. Assemble your sandwiches: bun, shredded BBQ chicken, a little bit of ranch salad dressing, green onions, and a sprinkle of crispy bacon bits.

Apple Cider Pork Tenderloin

We're big fans of pork tenderloin in the slow cooker. You don't have to brown it first—you just stick it in first thing in the morning, add your liquids, cover, and cook on high all day. That's it! By the end of the day, you have the most tender, ready-to-eat supper around. I'm telling you, pork cooked in the slow cooker is the best! On some evenings, we serve our pork over quinoa, but you could serve it on buns as a sandwich, over a baked potato, over rice, or over anything you want—or just eat it by itself! The apple cider gives the meat just a hint of fall flavor, and then we finish it off with chopped green onions. This meal looks fancy enough to serve to guests but is simple enough for even your busiest weeknights.

This recipe serves about six big portions.

INGREDIENTS

For the pork
1 (2 to 3 pounds) pork tenderloin (you might need two)
2 liters (about 8 cups) apple cider, divided (you can also use apple juice)
1 cup ketchup
1 tablespoon mustard
2 tablespoons Worcestershire sauce

For the quinoa
1 cup quinoa, rinsed under cold water and drained
1½ cups chicken stock or water
Extra virgin olive oil
Salt and pepper

Place the tenderloin(s) in the bottom of the slow cooker and then add 6 cups of apple cider. Cover and cook on high 6 to 10 hours (the longer, the better).

About 30 minutes to an hour before you're ready to eat, remove the lid and pull the meat out and into a bowl (it will be so tender and will fall apart immediately). Drain all of the liquid from the slow cooker. Place the meat back in the empty slow cooker and shred the meat using two forks. Next, add the ketchup, mustard, Worcestershire sauce, and remaining two cups of cider. Cover and cook on low for another 30 minutes to an hour.

Meanwhile, if you want to serve this over quinoa, add the rinsed quinoa and chicken stock to a small pot over medium-high heat and bring to a boil. Once it begins to boil, cover, reduce heat to low, and simmer for 15 minutes. (Do not remove the lid while it's simmering.) After 15 minutes, remove the lid and fluff with a fork. Drizzle in just a tiny bit of olive oil or a tablespoon of butter, and a nice pinch of salt and pepper. Serve the shredded pork tenderloin straight from the slow cooker over the quinoa.

Chicken and Mushrooms over Rice

Tonight's dinner is a classic slow-cooker meal. Layer your ingredients in the slow cooker, pop on the lid, let it cook all day, make some rice, dish out on plates, serve, and enjoy. This is a staple recipe you'll use over and over again. Bonus—you can use pasta, quinoa, or any other grain you like instead of the rice.

This recipe serves four.

INGREDIENTS

1 pound chicken breasts
1 (10 ounce) can cream of mushroom soup
2 cups fresh mushrooms, chopped (I use Portobello)
1 (1 ounce) packet dry ranch dressing mix
1 cup chicken stock or water
About 3 to 4 cups prepared rice for serving
Green onions for garnish, chopped

In your slow cooker, layer the chicken, mushroom soup, mushrooms, ranch dressing mix, and stock. Cover and cook on low for 6 to 8 hours or on high for 3 to 4 hours. When you're ready to serve, remove the lid and shred the chicken right inside the slow cooker with two forks.

To serve, add cooked rice to each plate and then ladle the chicken and mushroom mixture on top. Garnish with green onions.

Cheesy Chicken Pasta

I mean...sometimes, you just want to make a big old bowl of cheesy goodness, right? One night Andrew and Smith were gone, so the girls and I decided to indulge in a pasta supper. With chicken. And Ro-Tel tomatoes. And cheese. Because everyone knows queso is the best dip. When you turn it into supper, things are just magical! And bonus...it comes together in the slow cooker.

This recipe serves four to six.

INGREDIENTS

1½ pounds boneless, skinless chicken breasts

1 (16 ounce) package Velveeta cheese, cut into cubes

1 (10 ounce) can of Ro-Tel tomatoes

2 cups chicken stock

1 tablespoon chili powder

1 pound shell pasta

Green onions to garnish, chopped

Cilantro to garnish, chopped

In your slow cooker, layer the chicken, Velveeta, tomatoes, stock and chili powder. Cover and cook on low 6 to 8 hours or on high 3 to 4 hours. About 30 minutes before you're ready to serve, remove the lid and shred the chicken inside the slow cooker with two forks. Next, stir in the pasta. Cover and cook on high about 30 more minutes (or until the pasta is tender).

Ladle into bowls and garnish with green onions and cilantro.

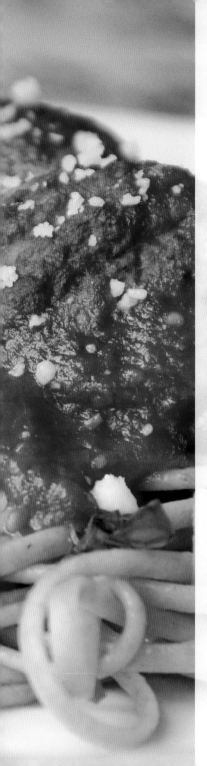

Slow-Cooker Spaghetti and Meatballs

My spaghetti and meatballs are a cinch to pull together when you use a bag of frozen meatballs from the supermarket. We love the frozen chicken or turkey meatballs, but beef or pork would work well too.

This recipe serves four.

INGREDIENTS

1 (1 pound) bag frozen meatballs
1 (28 ounce) can whole, peeled tomatoes (I love San Marzano)
1 (6 ounce) can tomato paste
1 (8 ounce) can tomato sauce
2 cups chicken stock
3 tablespoons Italian seasoning blend
1 pound spaghetti noodles, boiled to al dente
Parmesan cheese for garnish, grated
Fresh basil for garnish, chopped

In your slow cooker, add the meatballs, whole tomatoes, tomato paste, tomato sauce, stock, and Italian seasoning blend. Cover and cook on low for 6 to 8 hours or on high for 3 to 4 hours.

When you're ready to serve, remove the lid and lightly mash up the whole tomatoes with a wooden spoon inside the slow cooker. Toss in the cooked spaghetti noodles, mix, and then serve on plates with a garnish of Parmesan and basil.

Sweet and Tangy Meatballs over Rice

Okay, this recipe is so simple, you'll think it's wrong. The key is using a good quality frozen meatball. We love turkey meatballs, but beef, pork, or chicken also work.

This recipe serves four.

INGREDIENTS

1 (1 pound) bag frozen meatballs
1 (18 ounce) jar grape jelly
1 (18 ounce) bottle BBQ sauce
About 4 cups cooked rice (we use wild rice)
Green onions for garnish, chopped

Place the frozen meatballs in the slow cooker. Next, pour in the jar of grape jelly, followed by the bottle of BBQ sauce. Put the lid on your slow cooker and cook on low for 6 to 8 hours or on high for 3 to 4 hours.

To serve, add cooked rice to each plate, and then spoon the meatballs and sauce over the rice. Garnish with some green onions and dinner is done.

Something Sweet

Did you know you can use your slow cooker to make desserts? These sweet treats finish off any meal and are easily and quickly prepared in the slow cooker. Our blessed appliance isn't just for supper.

Gooey Butterscotch Cake

Apple Bread Pudding

Cinnamon Pumpkin Cake

Chocolate Blackberry Peach Cobbler

Peanut Butter Chocolate Cream Cake

Upside Down Strawberry Shortcake

Gooey Butterscotch Cake

In my opinion, butterscotch is that secret ingredient that everyone loves but doesn't use enough. This gooey little cake cooks up in the slow cooker and then makes the perfect dessert for any occasion. Who knew you could bake cakes in the slow cooker?

This recipe serves four to six.

INGREDIENTS

1 box yellow cake mix
1 (8 ounce) container sour cream
1 egg
½ cup water
2 cups butterscotch chips, plus a few more for garnish
Butterscotch ice cream topping to drizzle

Spray your slow cooker liberally with cooking spray. Then, in a mixing bowl, combine the cake mix, sour cream, egg, and water with a wooden spoon. Spoon this layer on the bottom of your slow cooker. Next, sprinkle the butterscotch chips across the top. Cover and cook on low for 2 to 3 hours. Remove from slow cooker and serve with a drizzle of butterscotch sauce and a few more butterscotch chips.

Apple Bread Pudding

One of our family's favorite desserts is bread pudding. I add just a few simple ingredients to my slow cooker, and *bam*, bread pudding is ready after dinner. You have to love that, right?

This recipe serves four to six.

INGREDIENTS

1 loaf challah or brioche bread, torn into pieces (you can also use 6 croissants)
1 stick (½ cup) butter, melted
2 cups applesauce
2 cups milk
4 eggs, lightly beaten
½ cup brown sugar
1 tablespoon cinnamon

Spray the slow cooker well with cooking spray. Layer the torn bread across the bottom. Pour the melted butter over the bread and lightly toss the bread in the butter to get everything coated. Next, in a mixing bowl, whisk together the applesauce, milk, eggs, brown sugar, and cinnamon. Pour this mixture over the bread. Cover and cook on low for 3 to 4 hours. Remove the lid and serve.

Cinnamon Pumpkin Cake

My very favorite flavor is pumpkin. Here is a yummy pumpkin cake that smells and tastes just like fall, cooked up in my slow cooker.

This recipe serves four to six.

INGREDIENTS

1 box yellow cake mix
1 (15 ounce) can pumpkin
1 egg
½ cup water
1½ tablespoons cinnamon

Mix all ingredients with an electric mixer and then spread in the bottom of a greased slow cooker. Cover and cook on low for 2 to 3 hours. Remove the lid and serve.

Chocolate Blackberry Peach Cobbler

I made a blackberry and peach cobbler...with chocolate. It's like the three best things in the world all in one bowl. Of course, you can swap out the chocolate cake mix in this little recipe for a yellow one if you prefer a more traditional cobbler. But my family? We love a good chocolate cobbler!

This recipe serves four to six.

INGREDIENTS

1 (10 ounce) package frozen blackberries
1 (10 ounce) package frozen peaches
1 box chocolate cake mix
1 stick (½ cup) butter, melted

Spray your slow cooker liberally with cooking spray. Next, pour in the blackberries and peaches. Sprinkle the cake mix on top of the fruit. Finally, drizzle the melted butter over everything. Cover and cook on low for 2 to 3 hours. Remove the lid and ladle your cobbler into bowls.

Peanut Butter Chocolate Cream Cake

The men in my family cannot get enough chocolate and peanut butter. This cake is rich and delicious!

This recipe serves four.

INGREDIENTS

1 (8 ounce) package cream cheese, softened
1½ cups creamy peanut butter
1 egg
1 chocolate cake mix
½ cup water

Lightly spray your slow cooker with cooking spray. Then, in a mixing bowl, beat the cream cheese and peanut butter together with an electric mixer. Beat in the egg, cake mix, and then the water. Pour this mixture across the bottom of your prepared slow cooker, cover and cook on low for 2 to 3 hours. Remove the lid and serve.

Upside Down Strawberry Shortcake

My Upside Down Strawberry Shortcake only has two ingredients. Two. You really can't get simpler than that!

This recipe serves four to six.

INGREDIENTS

1 (21 ounce) can strawberry pie filling
1 angel food cake, cut into bite-sized pieces

Spray your slow cooker with cooking spray, and then spread the pie filling across the bottom. Next, spread the angel food cake pieces across the top. Cover and cook on low for 2 to 3 hours. When you're ready to serve, remove the lid and ladle into bowls.

Recipe Index

Acknowledgments

There are so many people I want to acknowledge for making this book possible. Thanks go to:

First and foremost, my precious family, who ate nothing but slow-cooker meals for an entire summer as I worked on *Mix-and-Match Mama Simmers*. Andrew, Kensington, Smith, Ashby, and Madeley, you fill my life with more love than I ever thought possible. I love you all so very much.

My fantastic agent, Ruth Samsel, who encourages me, supports me, and tells me when I need to take a break and step back. Thank you. Your friendship means so much to me.

The amazing people at Harvest House that I'm so blessed to work with. Heather Green and Christianne Debysingh, you girls are rock stars, and I couldn't be doing this without either one of you.

The girls of F.C. I have shared more meals, more laughs, and more tears with you than I can count. You are the real super hero moms in my life, and I am blessed to call you friends. I love each and every one of you.

The amazing community of readers who show up to read my blog—I love you! You have enriched my life in more ways than I ever could have imagined ten years ago when I started this crazy journey. Thank you for the love, support, encouragement, and motivation you give me each and every day. I consider you friends.

And none of this would be possible without my Lord and Savior, Jesus Christ. My faith in the Lord is what sustains me each and every day. Born a sinner, saved by grace...He is my everything.

About the Author

SHAY SHULL is the author of the *Mix and Match Mama* blog and several cookbooks including *Mix-and-Match Mama Eats* and *Mix-and-Match Mama Kids in the Kitchen*. She writes about motherhood, adoption, world travel, holidays, organization, and, of course, yummy food. Passionate about coffee, traveling the world with her family, and Red Sox baseball, her greatest love is Christ. Shay lives in McKinney, Texas, with her husband, Andrew, and their four kids: Kensington, Smith, Ashby, and Madeley.

Connect with Shay on her blog at **MixandMatchMama.com**, or on social media as **@mixandmatchmama**.

Get More of Shay's Recipes for You and Your Family Too

ENJOYING ALL THE NEW SLOW-COOKER CREATIONS IN *SIMMERS*?

Here are some other cookbooks from the Mix and Match Mama
you and your family will love!

Inside this book you will discover more than 200 crazy good go-to
breakfast, dinner, and dessert recipes for every holiday, season, and month
of the year, as well as a helpful Tips and Tricks section
featuring "Baking Essentials" and "Grocery Staples."

Toasted Coconut and
Macadamia Nut Oatmeal

Buffalo Turkey Joes

Red, White &
Blue Trifle